Our Words, Our Revolutions

Di/Verse Voices of Black Women, First Nations Women, and Women of Colour in Canada

Edited by
G. Sophie Harding

Inanna Publications and Education Inc., Toronto, Canada

Published by: Inanna Publications and Education Inc.
operating as *Canadian Woman Studies/les cahiers de la femme*
212 Founders College, York University
4700 Keele Street, Toronto, Ontario M3J 1P3
Telephone: (416) 736-5356, Fax (416) 736-5765
Email: cwscf@yorku.ca
http://www.yorku.ca/cwscf

Printed and Bound in Canada
by University of Toronto Press, Inc.

Cover Design/Interior Design: Luciana Ricciutelli
Front Cover Art: Mickie Poirier, "Sun Woman," Oils, 16 x 12", 1997
Back Cover Art: Mickie Poirier, "Bed of Poppies," Oils, 34 x 26", 1997

Canadian Cataloguing in Publication Data
Main entry under title:
Our words, our revolutions: di/verse voices of black women, first nations
women, and women of colour in Canada

ISBN 0-9681290-4-8

1. Minority women – Canada – Literary collections. 2. Minority women –
Canada. 3. Canadian literature (English) – Minority
authors.* 4. Canadian literature (English) –Women authors.*
5. Canadian literature (English) – 20th century.*
I. Harding, G. Sophie, 1970-

PS8235.W7O997 2000   C810.8'09287   C00-930706-0
PR9194.5.W6O97 2000

In memory of Akidi Abe, who passed away February 2000.

Akidi, I took your death hard, too hard maybe. I know you're in a better place.
I grieve not for you but for me, for the world and what we have lost. I thank you
for the struggle, for fighting the last fight, for wanting more, for never surrendering.
A friend told me that death is not an end but a kind of birth.
I wish you happy new beginnings my sister.

Contents

Contributor Notes   91

Acknowledgements

The making of this anthology was a journey. Special thanks go to everyone who helped along the way.

Peace and love to the following people: to all those who submitted their work and shared a piece of their heart with me. To my friends and family, you have my eternal gratitude for your patience and encouragement. To organizations such as Native Women in the Arts and the York University Women's Centre who helped immensely in the process of pulling this book together. To the women at Inanna Publications and Education Inc., thanks for believing in my work and for making the publishing process a relatively painless one. To all those who "passed the word," encouraged people to submit their work, advertised for me and posted flyers for me—there would be no book without you.

We move forward together and the struggle continues.

—*Sophie*

Foreword

I wanted this anthology to be conducive to and indicative of some of the struggles of women of colour, Black women, and First Nations women. Thanks to the many women who have contributed to this book, we have achieved just that. This book expresses our pain, our laughter, our sweat, and our blood in our words. Each woman faces her own personal revolution everyday. Whether you are fighting to pay the rent, fighting to raise your children, fighting to maintain your sexual identity, fighting a disease, fighting a government, or fighting to stay alive it is important to stand up and be counted, always express your views, and never surrender. Historically it has been practice for all women to be lumped together as one group with the same pressures, the same problems and the same solutions. Our differences as women traditionally have not been celebrated. This book is about acknowledging our differences and celebrating our accomplishments.

For years, the western-liberal feminist movement has refused to adequately look at the differences among women. We have been knocking at doors yelling to be recognized as individuals and not as one cohesive group with the same ideas and aspirations—called "women." We, as Black women, women of colour, and First Nations women continually challenge this mind set. The writings of bell hooks, for example, have emphasized the plight of Black women and our struggle to move from the isolation of the margins of society to the centre where we belong. First Nations women and women of colour have historically used the gift of writing to let their voices be heard. First Nations women, through writing, have educated us about their culture and their history and expressed their sense of displacement and anger at living on their own land as second-class citizens. This writing enables all of us to understand our history and ourselves better, since it is First Nations land upon which we stand. Women of colour all over the world speak out through writings which let the world know that sameness is not acceptable or desired. All non-white women do not have the same-shared experiences or face the same oppressions.

It is impossible to cover in a forward, in one book, in one life-time the many subjects written and covered by Black women, First Nations women and women of colour; each of us is vast, unique, and special.

We bring to any table our personal histories, our own social and political ideas. This anthology is but a small drop in an extremely big ocean.

Voltaire said, "The pen is mightier than the sword." Through the use of the pen many women have found a weapon that is integral to personal and political revolution. In revolution, the *word* is what we have. Our pen becomes a tool that gives us light in the darkness and renews our souls.

The idea for this anthology came to me from my own personal experiences. Watching my friends and family turn to writing in times of trouble, in times of happiness and in times of great emotional and spiritual awakenings and or turmoil. It is through writing that we have found ourselves, that we have challenged ourselves, we have emerged into new selves, and we have discovered our old selves. Writing can take us many places—some of these places to which we wish to return, some of these places we would like to forget, and some of these places to which we aspire to ascend on a daily basis. For many women writing is also a way to become visible in a world where many of us are invisible.

There are women all over the world who suffer, who are fighting their government in order to have food, water, and shelter for themselves and their families. Women who are fighting for their basic human rights and face political oppressions, women who are jailed and tortured, women who are raped and have no place to turn. Many of these women, we don't hear their cries, they are silenced. Through writing we can know their stories. It is through knowledge that we begin to change some of what is wrong in society. My heroes in life, the people who have inspired me, who have changed my life with their words, many of them I discovered through the turning leaves of books.

And so, writing is a weapon in my fight. Many laugh and say that the women's movement is passé, feminism is dead and gone. Others feel that there is no more need for mediums aimed at giving a particular group attention and a chance to express their unique identity. I am not sure what feminism means to the rest of the world, but for me, feminism entails embracing difference in a world that praises sameness, feminism entails fighting all oppressions, poverty, and self-alienation. In the society I live in, these causes are far from passé. This is the war that I fight. My definition of feminism does not come from books or a particular movement. It comes from a society, an ancestry and a bloodline. I was born in Jamaica; I grew up in the country. The women who have affected my life and shaped who I am, are not children of the western-feminist movement. They are women who have not read or care to read about the western constructions of feminism or feminist discourse. Yet everything that I know about resistance, everything that I know about "keep on keeping on" and everything that I know about strength and integrity, I learned from a group of women from Jamaica. I applaud my mother, my grandmothers, and my ancestors for giving me their strength. It is their presence that guides my pen as I write in defense of all that I hold true and for all that I think is real. It is through them that I learned about feminism and it is their legacy that I wish to uphold. For all women globally who are in the revolution, who live, die, and exist to fight this struggle, this book is my salute to you.

—*G. Sophie Harding*

G. Sophie Harding

You ask me...

You ask who I am

I answer, I am a princess, a slave, mother of slaves, defender of the race, I am everything and I am nothing, I am invisible and I am a visible minority

You ask me where I live

I answer, I live among my ancestors, I live in Jamaica, I live in Canada, I live in Africa, I live in the ocean..... but I have no home

You ask me what's my name

I answer, I have been called many things, some I which I care to forget- the language that I speak is not my own, it doesn't celebrate who and what I am

You say to me, "tell me about you"

I answer, do you have an hour, a day, or a lifetime? I have many identities, many personalities, many viewpoints, many ambitions, many hopes, many dreams. What I can't say in words I try say without words, what I can't touch with my hands I try to touch with my soul, what I don't understand with my mind I try to understand with my heart, I am everything and I am nothing.

Reflection

I looked for a reflection of beauty
But found ugliness
I searched for a reflection of strength
But found weakness
I ached for a reflection of compassion
But found disillusionment
I sought a reflection of peace
But found chaos

I built dreams on your reflection
That turned into nightmares

I look to my reflection for beauty
To find the face of an angel
I search in my soul for strength
To hear the whispers of my ancestors
I listen to my heart for compassion
To feel the tears of the goddess
I probe my mind for wisdom
To hear the echo of my voice

I examine myself for peace
To find spirituality
To build my life on my dreams

Hoping to find gratification and empowerment

I look to my reflection....

Naomi North

I Have the Gift of Laughter

heart bursting
always pushing
my contending limits
gasping in the open air
every breath   feeling
inhaling the knowledge
of embodiment
I dance in the face of it all
the gift to be of light
to know the self
carries me through
the fragmentation of anguish.

in the knowing
the body speaks
touch illuminates
the shadows
crowding out my memories

I hold my conscience
as my anger holds me
and i stretch my rage
over years of wanting peace
and still
vigilance inspires determination

I will not be done.

Fractured

The brink of disaster
stretching across my mind
and piercing my heart
reaching   for   breath
fear mixed anguish
curving my sight

and all i want
is the freedom
bread of inner peace
that only
ignorance   or   revolution
could ensure

it's as though
i could break   like   glass
like a promise   not   kept

Rolanda Chavett Kane

Candle in the Dark

They killed the mind.
So we restored the soul.
They tried stealing the heart.
But the spirit was too strong.
They turned out the light,
but our view was stronger.
We saw through the darkness.
Through the darkness of what
some might call nothing
comes the shadow of hope.

THE FIVE CHARACTERISTICS OF THE POEM
CANDLE IN THE DARK

1 The body represents the nation of its people.
2 The flame represents our spirit of everlasting life.
3 The light represents our balance as a race and as a nation of living
   beings.
4 Its light represents an aura of universal love and grace.
5 Together we form an amnesty for all persons of colour.

Rolanda Chavett Kane

The Sunlight To My Shine

She is what I am. I am what she is.
She is me and I am she. She is the
path of sunlight to my shine.
We are not one without the other.
We share the gift of each other.
At times unseen, unspoken.
We are the start of each other's
creation.
We are the destiny, the starting points
of the beginning of our end. Life has
started and death shall not end the
pathway which we shall share.
She is the path of sunlight to my
shine.

In loving memory of my mom, Mrs. Madeline Suella Kane.

Rolanda Chavett Kane

Nature

They said that nature is beautiful,
beauty,
where must we look in order to see?
They say the ocean is deep, but how tall
must we stand in order to see?
Nature is beauty and beauty is free,
freedom of its beauty escapes within me.

Rolanda Chavett Kane

This Land

In the wilderness of my mind I stop and rake.
In the wilderness of my drink I stop and think.
In the freedom of my living I've taken the
time to learn from each and all my mistakes.

Valerie Wood

Love's Miracle

Before that first cleansing breath,
Of a miracle.

Rings in the ears,
Of creation.

Life's dance is played in the heart,
Of a couple's love.

Joy swims throughout her, out of this union
Of two, a journey of one has begun.

In this loving sheltered place,
Of warmth and darkness.

Grows the fruit,
Of love's desire.

Listening to the heart beat of the one who gives,
Of herself selflessly.

The two united, together wait for the signal,
Of time.

The magic of tomorrow,
Out of that love.

Without regard to the comfort,
Of herself.

It begins, a miracle
Of a great magnitude unfolds.

That cleansing first breath,
Of a miracle is drawn.

Valerie Wood

Fantastic Journey

A journey of a thousand steps begins with one
One person alone
Not a city makes
A city hides in its blossom the infancy humankind
Humanity belies its existence
The lone voice of reason falls on deaf ears
A tree falls
A new stronger life forges upward
Prayers hurled toward a deity that knows of everything
Winds echo in canyons created by unseen forces
Skyscrapers stretch into the sky blocking out the light
Blocking the light to hungry hands stretched out
Body gnarled asking why
Life continues moving forward
In a blink of a weary eye, light flashes
We are anew
An act of kindness washes away our sins
Rejoice
Through the birth of a babe
We are innocent again
Forward humanity marches
A fantastic journey begins

Life's Dance

Life's reflections,
Look back at us,
From a pond of still water,
The water that is life blood,
Revealing truths long buried,
We stare back,
Locked in stale mate,
Winds blow,
Rippling the image,
Waves crash against the shore,
Changing the contours of life,
We face these changes with defiance,
Changes bring new growth,
Giving way to meaning,
We find ourselves on a path to …
Peace becomes our partner,
The search for ourselves is lost,
Along the path we stop,
Look into water,
We see only ourselves,
Not who we want to be,
But as we are looking back at us,
Tomorrow will bring new winds,
From a new direction.

Neeta Singh

On a summer night

Sky's haemorrhage
Tragic footlights
Midnight madness
Silent footfalls
Rustling leaves
Repeated odours
Howling apparitions
Drugged watchmen
Tender words
Forgotten memories
Walking shadows
a known alienation

Neeta Singh

An apocalyptic fire
constantly threatens
Deep insecurities
transmute into actions
There is an organic aesthetic,
a tracking of impulse and causation
We are exhausting
the realm of effects
We are crying
on the border of our patience
The best of us are standing on tiptoe
The psychiatry of living is on.

Lisa Nicole Tai

The white kids call, "Hey China girl!"
and mimic voices from kung-fu movies.
Sometimes they like my long, black hair;
they say it makes the white boys stare.
I look just like the Chinese girls,
they're quick to let me join the circle
but I don't know their motherland
and I'll never fully understand.
The black girls call me chinee gal
and wonder how I know those island songs.
They judge me by my chinkee eyes
but I, often, take them by surprise.
I am who I am, and I can't change
my blood lines, I can't rearrange
Though some of you might think I'm strange,
above all, I am human.

She (original)

Sexy sway of shapely hips,
Witty words pass luscious lips,
Vicious comebacks, sudden quips,
Cool and deadly fingertips.

She can hold you in captivity
or let your spirits flow freely
like intrinsic lines of poetry —
Devour you entirely
(if yuh mess wid she)

Lingering scent of sweet perfume,
Her entrance to a crowded room,
A flower in the height of bloom,
She can save your soul or seal your doom.

Sensuous kisses, lipstick stains,
Beautiful faces matched with brains,
Shimmering, lovely locks of hair,
Curves and nerves, breasts smooth and bare.

A special world she has to share
Approach her slowly, if you dare
If you think you can handle the woman she is …

Sighs, thighs, her piercing eyes
Don't ever ask for compromise
Or contemplate female demise
But celebrate her power on the rise!

Kim Anderson

Tough

You've gotta' be tough

I remember him saying. That was the night he punched the bathroom
wall us standing in our middle-class blue-tiled bathroom, and then
there it was, little indented knuckle marks on the white shiny wall
above the blue tile causing us to giggle

nervously

and we didn't understand

*

The school yard seems as large as a football stadium like a roman
coliseum, kids crowds jeering yelling screaming cheering as the

little brown bomber

steps
into the ring.

*

I remember that,
he says

It wasn't even my fight

Fighting was a way of life.

We always used to fight after school—my sister getting teased

I'd be lined up after school, one fight after another and I would

go and fight.

she'd line me up.

Sometimes my brother would have fights and I would have to step in for him. He was too big, or it was unfair, *an unfair match*

and I would fight

*

On the way home
excited
sometimes

running alongside jumping

CSST!
don't speak that language

older brother knows
calm down, yes csst!

don't talk indian
Csst!

I remember that.

*

He is pushed, stumbles, breaks through the front of
and all of a sudden everyone is quiet in anticipation

fire and hungry and nasty little tense

and he looks up through his gentle embarrassment
meets the eye of the other

he knows he is going to fight.

*

I saw him coming and then

He punched me.

…and I started to cry.

the little brown bomber

*

the laughter
all around him rises up in his ears fills his head
swelling
and flows grows into rage hot through

he tenses and springs

*

I remember that day

that day that we had to go up in front of the class and state
our heritage

dad wouldn't let us go to Indian schools … it wouldn't be a

proper education

Heritage Day

and I went up there, everyone passing by, one by one, turning, standing in front of the class

You're Scotch, he'd told me, *You're Scotch*, again, your ancestors

"I'm a Scot"

and as the whole class laughed, I could feel my face turning red all the way up, I could feel it filling up

oh boy

I remember that.

*

They had to pull me off him.

Just like that, you see that concrete patio there,
just like that like those blocks I bashed his head   again and again
against the cement
I don't remember

Then they pulled me off him.

Kim Anderson

RCMP

"Rebellion 1885"

"With the settlers moving out west and the building of the CN railway,
   INDIANS were feeling increasing pressure to change their ways of
   life."

Large old photos, too, of black and white Mounties mustached standing
   beside smoldering fires and foggy bunches of Indians.

There she looks like she's looking at me. This was a person—what were
   her thoughts—is she really part of me?

"The RCMP answered the call of SIR JOHN A. MACDONALD and mobilized
   support."

*

"How long do you think this will take?" she asks.

The RCMP office has no one in it but her and her student. Clean, very
   clean.

"You just go and have a coffee, ma'm.
If ANYONE is going to do the waiting, it will be THIS YOUNG FELLOW
   here."

Waiting their turn.
Those bastards.

Arrest, court, what? Who do I know, who can I call?

She looks at the wall.

"REBELLION, 1885"

*

1995. More heroes
at a wedding.

Friend of a friend. An RCMP marriage. RED and tall he waits in the receiving line.

She sinks into her seat and wonders why am I here? She prepares as the BEST MAN prepares to make a speech.

The story of Sam McGee. A GREAT CANADIAN poem serves all occasions. Everyone knows and loves our history and heritage.

Modified and personalized. Now about an RCMP newly Red and newlywed, moving out west.

And the true test: meeting with the angry warriors.
But the Indians finally give in,
And drunken and spirited, he joins 'em 'cause he can't beat 'em...

Burning barely breathing she waits for the squaws to appear. Under the table it seems dark and safe.

When was it going to end?

*

YOU come with me, SON

—she feels like saying
excuse me can you please take down this billboard it offends me and it is full of lies.

But now he is on his way in
And she sits trying to look so honest and clean smiling confident.

"No problem, I'll just be sitting here.... No I don't mind."

Polite.
Vulnerability.

I'll just wait.

S-M-I-L-E

On the wall she wanders

CANADA-WIDE

WANTED

From out west. Is he Indian?

then...
CHILD MISSING

This one is. What are they doing on this wall?
*
The reception hall takes a strange hush in a very uncomfortable moment.

The poem has stopped momentarily with the poet's realization that this
is not proper *ethnic* etiquette.

I hope there are no Indians here He laughs sheepishly pauses

five hundred years.

Oh God, if only I were anywhere else but here. Just move me out.

In that second that was five hundred
She feels the rustling beside her
and then

the woman stood up.

I am an Indian

She said to the momentarily sober crowd.

my blood
my mother

I think I am going to die

Where is the bathroom I may cry
at any moment.

And all the pain of her years of shame

confusion and hidden pride

Wells and sticks, in her throat, unable to escape
In her eyes, in big pools,

And aches all over her body proud and sad.

When will this end? She is capable of no other thought.

How I love her.

How it hurts.

*

Standing now in the office, looking at the wall the tears come down in
   the life of the moment again.

And those bastards, the anger too, but too embarrassing now what am
   I doing here standing here crying in the office,

Waiting by the Louis Riel wall

and the WANTED

and the MISSING

With red red eyes of
God who will see me,

Pull it together and be tough she said

CLICK CLICK because now down the hall

here they come.

Dawn Burke

Be Encouraged

Do not knock yourself for the things you cannot change
Instead, find strength in the things you have mastered.

Never be restrained by uncontrolled circumstances of the past
But take charge of your future and make plans that will last.

At times you may be weighed down by past misfortunes
Or even tempted to believe that life is just a game of luck and chances.

But be comforted in the fact that luck and chances only materialize
When you prepare to take hold of opportunities as they rise.

So, make sure today's plans smooth the path for tomorrow
And do not dwell upon the things that will cause you sorrow.

Neither lean on the frailty of luck and chances
But rather on the security of the Almighty's promises.

Dawn Burke

Seasons of the Soul

Summer comes with such a splendor
All creation shows its praise
Flowers bloom, fruits ripen, birds sing
All things experiencing rebirth
All things are made anew

Summer's end ushers in autumn's colours
Gold red, crispy brown, sunshiny yellow
Autumn leaves come falling, falling
Peacefully lying in a final resting place
'Til winter's milky white, delicate snowflakes
Come cascading
Covering all they reach in fluffy softness
Followed by spring's revitalizing rainfall
Washing, showering, pouring, cleansing

Without human intervention or objection
The cycle continues o'er and o'er again.

Life is so much like nature's seasons
Changing constantly and surely with the passing of time
We too must face life's passing seasons
When there are days of summer-like splendor
All plans made falling into place
Obstacles faced, challenges conquered, goals surpassed

But, as surely as autumn follows summer and spring follows winter
We too must face our days of
Spring-like rebirth

Autumn-like falling
Summer-like passion
Winter-like coldness.

We too are faced with the seasons
The seasons of the soul.

Dawn Burke

See Me

Are you looking at me?
Yes, you.
Are you looking at me?
So now you think you've seen me and all that I am
Because you realize that I am black,
That I am different,
That I am the "other"?
Black for you is merely a category,
Lump 'em together you say.
They're all the same, aren't they?
Are they?

Stop! Look at me!
No, really, look at me.
Don't you get it? You're not seeing me.
Look long. Look deep. Look hard. See me.

Look beyond the dark pigmentation of my skin,
Look beyond the full contours of my lips,
Look beyond the rounded fatness of my nose,
Look beyond whatever creative way I choose to wear my hair today–
Nubian curls, afro, braids or just that "lo' flow."
SEE ME
See the person that I am
Not the person you perceive this skin colour to reflect.

I used to say they didn't matter–
Fake smiles and hypocritical relations,
Derogative names and the questioning gaze,

Criminalization and discrimination.
But they do matter.
I've suppressed the fear, the anger
But, deep inside they hurt
Eating away at me,
Demobilizing me,
Intimidating me.

No more!
I am breaking away
I want you to see me
See the person that I am
Do not judge me by the actions of others.

Yes I am black
But, there is more to me than the colour of my skin

SEE ME!

Vera M. Wabegijig

A Path of Discovery
Another Reason to Write

one time i was walking and i was passing by a tree   this
overwhelming feeling came over me,
i wasn't sure what it was
and i don't think i felt this way before

i stopped in front of that tree and looked up at it
it was a giant red pine   i said meegwetch
for what? i wasn't sure

i fasted that spring with some elders back home near
manitouland island   i learned during
those days that when you are rooted deep into
mother earth and creation,
your spirit feels creator's love

i asked how do you know?

you can feel it from creation   it comes from the soles of your feet
tingling   like an electric shock
and it moves throughout your body and fills you with
this immense feeling of love
a warmth over your body   and your spirit feels light

like from a tree?   and the elder nodded

that's when i learned that creation is alive and everything has a spirit
and when you are connected you pick up on this unconditional love
that is given so freely

i closed my eyes and my spirit took a journey …

it was dark but i was so warm   i felt like i was wrapped so tightly
it must have been the most comfortable i've ever been
i heard this beat   it was loud   like a water drum
and …
i began to pray
i began to sing
i began to dance
i heard a soft voice singing to me and i love this voice so much
but i did not know who it was because i couldn't see her …
my spirit came back to me and i still heard that beating,
i closed my eyes and it was the sound of my heartbeat,
it was my mamma's heartbeat i heard …
my spirit went back to her womb

i began to write about creation and this love
this beauty all around us
loving us
sustaining us …
when i create, when i write,
i remember to honour creation, i remember that
life is precious, that life is a journey, a path of discovery

and my path has brought me to this point of recognizing
how important it is to share my views and beliefs of life
there is too much negativity being spread
and not enough celebration

i choose not to dwell on the past
and feed those generational cycle abuses …
there are enough people spreading the word
(and i hope it is healing to them and others)
i think that there is not enough about the beauty
and to me, there seems to be more pointing the fingers
or just the same old talk
that has been going on for the last two decades

and no real solutions or new waves of thinking,
no ultimate healing in our nations ...

i know this work has to come out in order to open/free up
new ideas, new passions ...
it is healing ...
but i ask myself, where is it now
where was it when i needed to read something positive,
to help to stay alive, to want to stay in this world

and now that i passed that stage in my own life ...
my spirit, my fire is moving me
into a world of celebration, laughter and healing

a world where tricksters are alive, my granny is alive,
creation is alive, my ancestors are alive
this is where we come together to share our stories and
to drum, dance and sing

i honour this world that's been created in my own spirit world,
my writing world   this is where my magic comes from
this is where the circle is formed   this is where my baby is
this is where my partner is   this is where my family is

and this is where my life begins...

Mickie Poirier

The Believer

I have made you believe the story
Of a powerful Prince whose kiss
Will awaken your sleeping beauty
And you sleep,   forever waiting.

I have made you believe the story
Of MY destiny, MY actions,
MY goals to accomplish;
You deny yours,   forever waiting.

I have made you believe the story
Of MY needs, MY hungers,
Their place at the top of your list
You come last,   forever waiting.

I have made you believe the story
Of the penalties you'll pay
For your changes and violations
You obey,   forever waiting.

Sleeping, denying, deprived
And obedient,   you wait.
With my god and my gun
I have made you believe.

Roxane Tracey

For You

You told me
somebody hurt you
touched you hard and soft
in the dark

and all I can think of
is how your teardrops
must have sounded

just like tiny fists
as they hit the pillow
one
by
one

and how
in the night's shadows
those tears
must have rolled
down your cheeks
shoulders
arms
into your tiny fists

which stuck out
at the world
one
by
one

and all of this
because
you were a child
whose heart was quick to love
lungs too slow to scream

and all of this
because
the world has
no arms to
keep you safe
like it says it does

and all of this
because
teardrops crawl silently

and the tiny fists
of a child
cannot wake
the night

audra naomi diptee

The Darkest Night

as she sits in her
corner
with eyes closed
she remembers

how
one of them put his cock
in her mouth

while the other
lifted her dress
and rode the bitch to his glory

she remembers that night
because it was the darkest night
there was no moon
no stars
no god

for CC and MR, as always

audra naomi diptee

I am

Doh give meh no race,
no place,
no class,
no colour

I am what I am what I am.

Division all yuh fools
Make us less … not more,
Weaker … not stronger.

I am what I am.

Bishakha Chowdhury

Bijoya Images

Wimmin feeding
wimmin
Wimmin hugging
wimmin
Wimmin nourishing
wimmin

why then
the rest of the year
do we chatter and batter
about good housekeeping/good wife/good mother/
slut/bad cook/bad mother/too thin/too fat/
not good enough for my son?

i call upon each
mothersistergrandmotherdaughterauntgranddaughterloverfriend
to nourish each womyn
in our lives
physically, mentally, emotionally, spiritually
all through the year

Mooshum

Mooshum's the bull rider
On the porcupine ranch
Keeping me in line
On Indian time

Makes me wait
For granny's visit
Mooshum is a trickster
A Wesakechak with the berry basket

Kohkom is impatient
With Mooshum's moon game
Every month
He makes her late

I drink lots of tea
Think strawberries
Racing pregnant thoughts
Pray for the end of the moon

Laughing
Mooshum lets the porcupine go
Gives gran the berries
As he bull rides into next month

Lorraine Thomas

Retribution

You wear this blue suit
To serve and protect me
Against you I am astute
You take me into custody

This ride is rough
The back seat I'm in
This jewelery of handcuffs
Against my brown skin

Stare nails through bars
You're on the dominant side
Joking about the "Indian wars"
I stare back from inside

I think about Big Bear
My ancestral hero
You can cut my hair
But can't steel tomorrow

There will be retribution
Someday I'll carry the gun
Stalking a solution
For all the damage done

Tanya Cora

Handle with Care

cerebral heartbeat,
safety packed,
"handle with care"
stamp
blood-red warning.

pink insulation candy floss
— fibral matter
prevents crazed
pitter-patt collisions —
encounters rebound.

splinter-soft figurines
remain unharmed,
easter egg nested,
fragile,
in green frilly
pseudo grass.

mating rituals move
to new territory:

exploratory
solitary
companionship
confinement.

Marisa Rosalind Maharaj

My Declaration of Independence

All mine is myself.

Why would I
want to be with one
who shares my same
colour?
and that is all?

And why
would I want
to be with one
who sees me as
a shell – with exotic skin
unlike his own ...?

Either a shared shade
or various in variety
I MUST? Fall into your ARMS?
I cry, I scream
I declare NO!

Why should I be with
one
who neglects to see
my glow – my light –
my humour – my mind
MY beauty
Independent to myself
and

unique
I am me
not a
clone of culture
See me for who I am
or do not see me at all …

This poem is dedicated to my mom 'cause she taught me all about independence.

Randa Hammadieh

Guilt

From Andalusia birds resplendent in emerald and ruby sing to me:
Nothing is forgotten.

In twilight I dreamt the children of Sarajevo came forth from their graves. They cleft the earth asunder as the lilting olive branches stood witness. They joined hands and waded across the black oceans.

The children converged upon me at sunset and their cries reverberated reaching a frenzied pitch.

They drew me my jagged cowardly soul and shook it mercilessly, relentlessly

wave upon wave

I was brought to my knees by the howling of the living corpses of the ten thousand children

By twilight I had been made to witness a vision in which humanity was replaced

by birds that would not stop singing,
by birds that would not die,

And the children of Sarajevo walked forever onwards into the blazing sunset.

Rolanda Elijah

The Roundance

The speaker is done speaking.
Singers now move the centre.
Rattles shake to a humming waterdrum.
The lead singer's voice calls out.

Dancers move to the centre.
Our feet always recognize the song.
Children excitedly rush in too.
The inner circle has been started.

More feet find their way in unison.
Our outer circle has been started.
We too begin to move as one,
in the opposite way of the inner circle.

We are dancing.
As the first verse of song ends,
Our circle stops moving.   We pause.
I think about the roundance.

The waterdrum happily starts up.
Again, calling to attention rattles and feet.
We now begin moving clockwise,
and I think of the meaning of our dance.

I smile and I look down to my little girl.
I have been dancing since I was her age.
She is too small to dance on her own,
so I hold her hand tightly.

Grandmothers and grandfathers danced,
in the same way that I dance.
Now I watch my daughter dance.
The roundance: it is about continuity.

I have danced many times before,
but my thoughts cause me to lose step.
My child and I both lose our balance.
I help her to regain her footing.

I focus on maintaining my step.
Still I am thinking about the roundance.
What does our dance mean?
I watch the people as they move.

I feel the person kicking inside me.
Tiny flutterings of aniticipation.
Dancing to ancient rhythms of peace.
Roundance: a new heartbeat of friendship.

All feet move in sync. We are one.
Roundance: it is about oneness.
In roundance we forget our differences.
Roundance: there is hope for the future.

Amused, as I watch my daughter
reach for a little boy's hand.
She is a friendly child.
The boy pulls back in shyness.

The inner circle moves clockwise.
Our circle moves counter-clockwise.
We reflect the polarity of our world.
Roundance: balance and completeness.

In our prayers we pray for one mind:
"'Akweku ushka tsi' Atwahwenu:ni Akwahnikula.'"

Unity is an important part of life.
Roundance: our bodies reminded of unity.

I see my daughter getting tired.
I pick her up and dance with her.
She is happy with her new view.
Now she can see everything.

We dance and the song is finally over.
I'm glad because my arms are sore.
I put my daughter back down.
Everyone moves away from the centre.

The workings of a universe.
Roundance tells us who we are
and how we all fit into the world.
Roundance: it is a simple truth.

These are my thoughts.
I am walking from the circle,
and my daughter is at my side.
The roundance has served its purpose.

Two in One

At times…
I want to hug you
At times…
I wish to kiss you
At times I want to talk to you
Most times I miss you.

Sometimes I can hug you
Sometimes I really kiss you
Sometimes I still miss you
These times I think I
might love you.

I am fascinated by your wit
Enchanted by your humour
Melting in your gaze
and boiling at your touch.

I am afraid of everything that
I am feeling
Frightened that I want too
much.

Marguerite

Breathe

One woman smiles,
Remembering the
One woman who breathes;
tempering,
The thought of one woman
soon to be born…
A daughter
in this world of women
Thinking, working, breathing
Life into each other.

Doreen Gaiyadéyéné: s Silversmith

Surviving the Hunger
(work in progress)

"Ah choo...it's cold!" she whispered while taking in a deep breath.

"Who's still in there anyway?" the old man asked in the Cayuga language.

"I don't know," came the reply in *Onondaga* from his partner. The sound of water splashing could be heard in the pantry room that doubled as a washroom where the family washed their hands or took sponge baths. The old man got up from his chair in the kitchen and sauntered over to the pantry to see who it was. "Oh ... it's you. I thought I was getting haunted," he said, half-smiling.

"*Dis sa dri heh, O:nen* (hurry now) or you'll be late for school," he added.

Standing near the old wooden stand that held a wash basin with water in it, the seven-year-old girl shyly looked up at her *ha:ni* (father) as he turned away to go back to the kitchen.

She was *hoo gégoo ny* (bare-naked) and standing on a towel so as not to get the floor wet. She used her little brown hands to scrub her small belly. After she was done, she washed her legs and feet very quickly. She dried herself off with a towel hanging from a nail. The scent of soap hung sweetly in the air. The girl then got dressed, carefully tucking her blue flannel shirt into her black slacks. She heard the footsteps of her mother approaching the room.

"*Dis sa dri heh, O:ner*. You'll be late and your teacher will be yelling at me, wanting to know why you're always late," her *:knoha* (mother) chided as she handed her a blue cotton fall jacket.

"And don't forget your lunch too." Her mom was fluent in both Cayuga and Onondaga and would often alternate between these two (of six) dialects of the Six Nations.

"Okay," the small girl remarked after she was done putting on her blue patched-up socks and black shoes. "At least, they're clean, " she told herself as she looked at her old, faded clothes. "I'll just tell them that. Yep, that's what I'll say."

The children at school whose parents were a little better off, though still considered poor by white standards, always taunted her about the second-hand clothes she wore since she started classes at Number Eleven School. Some of their parents had "high steel" jobs and others were teachers.

She had one last look in the mirror while standing up straight and putting on her jacket. A shiny nose and a glimpse of pride and innocence that she wore on her face rebounded back to her dark eyes. Her shoulder-length dark hair was neatly combed. She left the room, grabbed her lunch off the table and scooted across the living room to the front door. "See ya' later alligators," she called out to her parents as she walked out.

"Way ya hó …way ya hó …way ya hó …way ya hó …," the little girl sang as she headed up the gravel road towards school which was three or four miles away. "Way ya hó …way ya hó …way ya hó …way ya hó …way ya hó …" she repeated as the *Eskanyé ginah* (women's shuffle dance song) rode on the fresh autumn wind. There were no buses running along her route. So like all the children who resided along the River Range Road and area, she had to walk to and from school. Commando started Grade 1 when she was seven because her mother felt it was too cold in the winter for any of her children to walk the long distance to their classes.

"Rainwood? You're late again!" Commando's grade-one teacher berated her when she showed up fifteen minutes late in the classroom. She was addressed by her last name whenever her teacher was upset with her. "Now, go and sit down!" She was embarrassed. A few classmates snickered and giggled. "Class, simmer down!" they were told. Quiet was restored and Commando took her exercise book from her desk and began writing down the foreign English words from the blackboard.

At morning recess, Commando stood alone outside by the green and white building facing Cayuga Road. It was connected to her class by a long hallway and also housed the grade four class. She could hear the other children hollering with delight as they played on the school grounds. No one asked her to play with them and this made her sad.

They shunned her because of the way she was dressed. "You're a witch, Commando!" a boy from grade four said. "Look at your clothes, they're ugly and faded," he taunted while giving her a shove. "At least they're clean," she said through tears as she pushed him down. He began crying, got up quickly and ran away. Two other boys who were with him laughed and shouted at her, "No wonder they call you Commando!" The bell rang and recess was over.

She stood there for a minute, listening to the sound of her heartbeat. Finally, she returned to class and was again scolded by the teacher for her tardiness.

At lunch time, Commando sat alone eating bannock and lard with salt. She didn't have store-bought bread to go with lunch meat like her classmates. The oranges and apples they had for dessert were out of her league. She could only dream of having them. When there was no food at home, she would go to school hungry. When lunchtime rolled around and she didn't have lunch, she stepped outside to dream in her little hide-out. She daydreamed of a time when there were only *Óngkwe hón: we* living off this land. In that world, she was loved and accepted. There was no poverty or hunger. It was also where people shared and cared. Only the sound of the bell would bring her out of her dream and she would return to class.

She watched the time tick away the afternoon. About half hour before class was let out for the day, her heart sped up out of fear of being attacked by some classmates on her way home from school. These physical and verbal assaults occurred after each school day. Commando sought protection from her sister, Dee, who was in grade two and her brother, Bob, who was in grade three. However, there were often five or six boys ganging up on them. They were pushed around and hit or splashed with water from a mud puddle. When her brother and sister were both absent from school, she was forced to fend for herself. She would come home muddied up from being thrown on the ground. When winter rolled around, her clothes would be soaking wet from being thrown in the snow banks. The attacks stopped only when the gang reached their homes on River Range Road.

Commando lived about two miles from the white government-imposed boundary line—a division between Six Nations of the Grand River Territory and the "white side" towards the town of Caledonia,

Ontario. Traditional Longhouse families, like hers, do not believe in boundaries.

Her *:knoha* had the odd job of cleaning two homes at Six Nations and one in the white town which earned her two dollars a day for each one she cleaned. When she got paid, she went to the Hill's store at Beaver's Corner to buy flour and lard to cook bannock for her family.

One time, when it had been four days since her family had anything to eat, Commando sat on the floor in the kitchen weak and "pale-faced" from hunger watching her *:knoha* cook bannock on the wood stove which also served as her family's source of heat during the winter. When her mother announced that the bannock was ready, Commando jumped up and was the first one to the table. She declared, "Gimme some! I'm the hungriest!" May Rainwood looked down at her daughter and said, "Don't you think the others are just as hungry? They haven't eaten in a while either." But Commando was adamant that she was the hungriest. She said, "The worms (hunger pangs) in my stomach are beginning to talk. Listen." Her *:knoha* played along with her and said, "I guess they're grumbling too. Your *ha: nih's* cross. He's hungry." In the matriarchal society of the Six Nations, children follow their mother's clan. Commando's clan is Killdeer, but they follow their father's Cayuga nation.

When Commando's father walked into the kitchen, her mother teased him. "You're of the Wolf Clan, that's why you're so cross."

In the evenings, Commando's mother told her children about her house-cleaning job in Caledonia. The old couple at one job were nice to her. They had fourteen cats and dogs and were called "dog lovers" by the locals in the area. One of the dogs, Queenie, was allowed to sit at the table with them at breakfast time and have her own plate of food. One evening in particular, the younger ones gathered around the stove with her to hear that story. "I walked that six miles down that dusty road today, until I came to the pavement on the outskirts of *gy dónnée* (Caledonia)," began their mother. "My feet were red and blistered. Oh, they hurt. I didn't let the white couple know I was in pain. I started this morning by taking a big heavy rug outside with the help of the husband." Commando sized up her *:knoha's* shoulders on her four-foot-eleven-inch frame and her small, cracked hands. She thought of her mother as a hero who could weather any storm.

"Oh, he was useless," her mother continued. "He barely lifted it. He went back inside to lay on the couch, just huffing and puffing. I thought he would die." She paused briefly to stir up the wood in the stove with the iron poker. Commando, Dee, Bob and Donny, the youngest, waited attentively, looking into the fire.

"You'll pee in your pants if you stare at the fire before going to bed," their mother said. All four sets of eyes focused shyly on her, but they couldn't read her face. She looked so serious they all agreed with her, and her smile returned.

"Hey Commando, I'm going to tell you something. You know how the white people call us Ónkwé hón: wé 'dirty Indians'? Well, that 'white' house was so dirty, it took me the rest of the aftenoon to clean it. The washroom especially was real dirty. So, they don't know what they're talking about when they call us bad names. But we got to eat, so I put up with their shit one day every week." Commando's eyes sparkled with pride for her :knoha. That night Commando and her family went to bed full even if it was just bannock, lard, and salt.

Her mother also worked at a canning factory and at an electrical plant in Dunnville and surrounding towns like Simcoe. The children were left at home in the care of their father who had lost his job at the Domtar mine in Caledonia because of his drinking. He used to mine gyproc but would blow his paycheque on booze in the hotel or at the liquor store. So, their mother used to try to go to meet him at the Exchange Hotel in town before he spent all his money. These times Commando and her brothers and sisters would ask for a pop and a gadget with a little plastic container full of soapy water, and a ring with a handle. After dipping the ring in the soapy liquid, they blew bubbles through it.

Commando's dad was a man with disabilities. He had low vision in one eye as a result of a chip of rock striking it when he was a miner. He also had a ruptured belly from lifting heavy loads at the mine. But he was afraid of surgery. He didn't trust the white doctors in Ohsweken at the Lady Wellington Hospital.

Commando loved it when her whole family stayed at a farm in Stoney Creek picking what fruit was in season; like cherries, plums, prunes and apples. She enjoyed the months of July and August the most because her family was together, subsisting day to day on whatever

67 |

they made picking fruit. It was one of her happiest times. Commando even managed to save enough money to buy a new pair of pants or shoes at the "swap shop" for school in the fall.

During the winter, her father sometimes trapped animals such as rabbit and muskrats near the Grand River. Usually, he got their mother to walk with him through the moonlit forest to the traplines. They'd be all bundled up, her mother following her six-foot husband, occasionally shoving him in a teasing manner.

One day, Commando's mother announced to the family, "We can't eat rabbit no more because they are sick. The rabbits have green and white spots on their bellies. All the animals in the forest are sick because of the white men bringing poison around here. They made them sick. One day the creeks and rivers will be spoiled by them too."

Commando sat teary-eyed because it meant that she could no longer fish with her dad at the Grand River in the spring. They didn't have anything fancy to catch the fish; just a line, sinker and fishhooks that her father bought at the hardware store in Caledonia. For bait they used worms from their land. She loved it when her mother cooked "the catch of the day." It was dipped in flour and put in a big, black frying pan with lard boiling in it over the wood stove. In the oven there would be bannock to go with the fish.

Sure enough, what her :knoha told them that day came true, and Commando could no longer drink the water from the stream near her cousin's house on River Range Road. Before, she had been able to see the pebbles at the bottom. Then, the water was absolutely clear and pure. She would lay on her belly and sip the water if she was thirsty on her way home from school. The stream ran from the Grand River, snaking its way across the road into the forest behind her cousin Saul's log house. It continued across the Cayuga Road on the concession near her other cousin's house. In the winter, the children played "shinny" on the frozen stream near Number Eleven School.

Quite often, when it was bitterly cold in the winter, the Rainwood family cut through the bush on a path they beat on their way to and from school. The huge old trees afforded them safe passage from the biting wind and freezing temperatures. The forest also served as a barrier from the attacks of the other kids, who didn't dare follow them into their refuge. When she was safely walking with her brother and sister,

Commando enjoyed the sounds of the forest, like the crackling of the trees rubbing against each other and swaying in the brisk wind.

Many mornings, the trio left the sleeping owls in the trees undisturbed. Sometimes they'd see bats napping there. Commando often called up to them. "Did you have all night *Ogee:wé* ? That's why you're sleeping now?" *Ogee:wé,* (a feast for the dead and big snake which took place once in the fall and once in the spring) used to last all night. A long time ago her *:knoha* had told her that. Now *Ogee:wé* takes place in the afternoon and lasts only until around seven o'clock in the evening. Commando likes the sense of community as the people of the Longhouse carry out their duties of the ceremonial cleaning of their friends' and relatives' graves. Everyone is helpful and cheerful. The sacred ceremony continues the next day at *Ganósé:s* (Longhouse).

The winter months were the hardest on the family. The monthly government handout of six dollars a child helped out a little. Of the eight children, only the six youngest qualified. Thirty-six dollars had to be stretched out for the family of ten, which included their mother and father. The payout is nicknamed "baby bonus." Commando's two older brothers, Noman and Peter, worked occasionally at a farm across the boundary line on River Range Road. In return, they received fresh cow's milk, a half sack of potatoes, and some lard.

Every two years in the winter, Commando's parents hired a neighbour to take them to Brantford, Ontario—a small city adjacent to Six Nations of the Grand River Territory. The purpose of their journey was to pick up five dollars per person in the family from a government office. The money came from a war chest set aside for members of the Cayuga Nation. It is the British government's way of saying "thank you" to them for assisting, as allies, in the hard-won bloody battle against the Americans, and also to say "thanks" for helping the British steal their land. Their parents had to present white tickets with the family's name and Nation written in black to the people who dole out the fund. Her mother kept the tickets neatly tucked in a small black leather purse.

Commando's *:knoha* told her children of a time long gone by when her great-great-grandparents helped the Aboriginal people on horseback by making sure that they had enough baked corn in their satchels. It was for the long journey to join the British in their fight against the

Americans to establish Canadian sovereignty. She told how her great-great-grandparents sang and danced traditional war dance songs in support of the *Óngkwéhón:wé* who went to war. During that battle, her mother was told, there was a big dark man who came out of the clouds to blow the American soldiers into the river. Commando enjoyed the stories her mother told.

A little stir of excitement occurred on the one day of the year when Commando's parents picked up the *Ó wisda* (money). It meant that she and her family could enjoy rare treats like oranges, bananas, and salt pork or back bacon to go with their bannock. The children huddled together as they waited at home, pressing their little brown faces against the frosted-up window panes. Their dark, hungry eyes searched the laneway from behind the melted peepholes on the windows. Every so often one of their tummies protested with hunger pangs.

From her bed, the night before, Commando had asked *Shóng-waiadihs:on* (Creator) to take her and the family's lives so they wouldn't suffer anymore. She often heard it said at *Ganósé:s* (Longhouse) that in the land of the Creator there is no hunger, pain, or any judgements placed upon *Ongkwéhón:wé*. She had looked out the window and up at the crisp, wintry night sky. Grandmother moon caressed her sad face which was saturated with warm teardrops. Soon after, the little girl slipped into the dreamland of the Creator.

This is a work in progress, excerpted from the author's book, "It Just Is..." Stories from the "Bush" and Gwanoha (Our Mother, Our Earth).

Irene Young

Walk With Me

I have traveled your path
It brought me despair
It took away my inherent values & beliefs
Because I had trust in you
From that I gained disrespect for other nations & myself
Because I thought I had gained a rightful place in your world

I learned how to cope with daily complexities
Trying to survive in a foreign environment
Unlike my familiar, safe & understanding community
From that I learned how to depend on alcohol

I truthfully tried to master your native tongue so unlike mine
Thus I came across manipulation
I also stumbled upon greed
Doing away with caring & sharing as I was so accustomed to
Until I became assimilated & lost

You said I needed to be saved
I believed

I believed …
When I emerged like a butterfly
Wings still wet & the uncertainties of how to use the wings
Still today, I struggle with the cocoon
Things I cannot let go of or do not want to let go of

Irene Young

I cried to my Creator
There I found understanding & love
I cried to the universe
There I came to know my Grandfathers & Grandmothers
I gained self-worthiness

Take my hand
Walk with me as your sister
We will walk quietly & peacefully together
On Mother Earth

Accept me as I have accepted you
For we are of the same creation
We have similar trials & tribulations
Together we will share our inspirations with joy & happiness
As we continue our journey together

At the end of the day
We can say we tried....

Heather MacLeod

Dead Birds

The last year of her death, she walked the hills
filling a cloth bag with dead birds. She brought
dead crows home, spread their wings across
the work table, cut them off, black wings
in woven baskets by her bed.
In the first year of his adolescence,
while playing with his prized pellet gun,
he shot a whiskey jack; the bird
lay on the ground, struggling and scrambling,
life very difficult to let loose.
I dreamt of that bird for years
struggling in my hands, though he never did.
My sister is inside me with her black wings
and my brother with his gun at my feet
and I have dead birds in my hands.

Heather MacLeod

What I Have Left is Imagining

I used to live in the arctic,
but I left so often my leaving
became un-noticed, an event
which slipped away devoid of celebration.

I used to live in the arctic,
thought I was a boomerang,
my point of origin the north,
but I grew up, here, in the Cariboo
with bit and bridle, Bay and Appaloosa,
instead of inukshuk and ulu, Char and Whitefish.

I used to live in the arctic,
found my ancestors' footsteps in the Northwest Passage
trailing behind Franklin, and found
what it meant, for me, to be Métis.

I used to live in the arctic,
a place where my Indian blood
found room to live in, elliptical
it moved within me, solid as snow,
smooth and clear as the first layer of ice
over the waters of Great Slave.

I used to live in the arctic,
and what I have left is imagining,
imagine me talking to you
frost trailing out with my breath;
pretend I speak sounds in the shape of syllabics,
say thank you in Dogrib, pretend I cry in Cree.

Heather MacLeod

Red Earth

My grandfather saw a zebra loose
in the streets of Germany, it was the only
war story he'd ever tell. He fell into Germany,
a paratrooper, like gumball candy.
Sometimes, in my dreams the zebra
comes to me confused by the gunfire,
the smoke, and I put my hands over his eyes
and I tell him, *Don't cry, Grandpa, don't cry.*

I travelled to Guatemala from the Arctic;
the hills were covered in dust
which ran like red clay, rust smudged
my hair, caked itself around my sandals,
between my toes like henna stains,
the texture of it marked my body.
When I came home the Cree elders
gave me tea, one of the elders told me,
we are imprinted by animals,
the gods move beneath their shapes,
into our dreams, smiling, the spirits play with us;
laughing, the gods mark who we are,
brand our flesh and experiences to the bone.

In Guatemala, the red earth stained me;
I wanted to run and kick up the earth,
an orange flame of saffron; I wanted land
to cover not only the bottom of my feet,
but the crevices between my fingers,
to brand me like a tattoo. I wanted

the soil to move across me like a map.

In my wallet is a photograph of my grandpa
taken in Berlin at the end of the war.
His helmet rests in his hands and his face
is striped with mud, the soil of Europe
imprinting his features with remorse

Heather MacLeod

The Prayers of Islam

Because I look White and because
I am mostly that; Scottish blood
in my face, eyes, hair, and hands
colours my flesh like ripe apricots,
and because of this, my small acre
of Cree blood settles in my feet.
The soles and callouses whisper
to me like lavender left on my pillow.
My Cree blood dreams of all the worlds
I have tracked my weight over and across;
oceans carry the indent of my heel
to my toes. Once outside of Izmir
in a two-door, burgundy rented hatch-back
I made a list of my body—what belongs
where; last night I dreamt myself walking
over the flagstone streets of Taksim
and Sultanahmet. I let those moments
roll together until they sit spinning side
by side, oval and smooth as eggs.
My feet carry back the smell of chestnuts
roasting in the chill of winter outside
the Blue Mosque; brown paper bags filled
with cold, salty popcorn. My feet remember
the cobblestone in the side alley on the way
to Köy Café, and the worn steps to the fitas,
my feet carry me back to Turkey, the splash
of Turkish over my skin and the prayers
of Islam travel across the oceans dance
over my body and sing to my ears.

When I was sitting outside Izmir
thinking of the way I saw my Cree blood,
inherited from my mother, living just beneath my feet
I imagined my heart and saw it, as if it would rest
in my hands, the pump of it, the shape of it
like my fist. I imagined holding it against my chest,
imagined my feet pulled up, bare and resting
against the black vinyl of the dashboard,
and I recognized my heart wasn't Cree;
my heart wasn't, like my feet,
inherited; it was foreign. To me, it was foreign.

Heather MacLeod

I Am Only Canadian

Turkey makes me less than what I was;
in Canada my family tree spirals its way
through Wounded Knee and the Highlands,
but in Turkey I am only Canadian.
Cree and Scottish Grandmothers disappear
in the fog from the Bosphorus Strait.
The past thirty years which I have felt
pull and twist me, suddenly lie behind,
a long drive on an autumn road in the prairie.
I am hiding too much in my hands, afraid
to show this man what I'm made from.
I feel myself unwinding, nothing fits anymore.
The vastness of Canada allowed me space
to move in, time to grow, but Turkey
forces me into tight double knots of silk.
A smallness which leaves me naked.
I have too much to hide, and must
hold it all in the cup of my hands.

I Am the First A.F.R.I.C.A.

I am the first!
I am a Mother.
My children call me by My Name
My children call me Africa.
I am not West or East
I am not North or South,
My name is Africa.
They all call me Africa.
Even my sisters and cousins'
Siblings.
Because that is my name.

My sisters America and Europe,
My cousins Russia and Asia,
All of you were born after
Me,
My sisters you were born;
But never saw Our Mother!
I fed you milk and honey.
I taught you wisdom.

How! Now you feed me war and death?
You bundle me in poverty and disease.
Come and find out; what Our Mother
Said on her death mat.
Mother died at twin-childbirth,
You America and Russia
Her un-identical twins.
Listen Mother had a Will.

Looking for nothing you go
In search of what you cannot get,
I Africa have the Will! Not
The Moon, Mars, Neptune or
Call it what you please.
Remember, Our Mother's
Name is ALOBO EARTH.

I am very proud ,
Let me tell you what I have!
The Pearl,
The Cradle of fresh river water,
King of the jungles is my pet
Elephant dinosaurs largest;
Only remaining creatures.

My daughter Egypt opened
Civilization for you all.
Where is my Gold Coast
What happened to my
Ivory Coast ?
I didn't need Fort Jesus,
For here you shamelessly bundled my children
Into Slavery.

I Africa have a heart
Pure in forgiveness.
Your disgusting attitude
torments my children.
Reward me PEACE not WAR not DEATH.
And I'll feed, shelter and
Clothe My Children.

Come to me ask for Mother's Will;
Do not fear I am not backward;
I am only a first–born,
I am unselfish

But, Loving and Caring.
Remember you took my share of The Will,
Ruined my optimism,
My children are pessimistic for your attitudes.

Satisfying your power hunger
You,
Declared me Bankrupt.
Still I will show you what
Mother wants of You and Me.

All of you are pieces of
Me AFRICA.

A – America (North and South),
F – France,   R – Russia, I – Ingland
and Ireland, C – Canada and
Caribbean, A – Asia and
Australia = AFRICA.

Notisha Massaquoi

Writing Resistance

If we stand tall it is because we stand on the backs of those who came before us. —African proverb

I am writing in the hope that I can resolve the contradictions and conflicts in myself that newly-acquired knowledge often brings. I write in resistance of the formal system of education I have chosen to immerse myself in. I write to reevaluate and validate who I am and where I am situated in this system, something I am forced to contemplate as a Black student attending a predominantly white university.

I remember entering the Graduate School of Social Work for the first time, feeling both a sense of excitement and relief. Relief that I had actually found my way to the faculty, both literally and figuratively. I had recently quit my job, said goodbye to family and friends, and moved to a new city to begin the next phase of my life as an independent, confident graduate student. It seems I was so excited by this new confidence that I misread my schedule and had arrived an hour early for my orientation session. Looking around for something to amuse myself with for the next sixty minutes, I noticed a very prestigious-looking wall of photographs. Laid out in front of me were the former students of the program who were being rewarded for their accomplishments with the public display of their images for all posterity. I scanned each of the graduating classes looking for those who had gone before, those who looked like me, those who could understand my choice to leave secure employment for the pursuit of higher education, those who could support me in a system that does not provide any safety or space for particular members of society.

The wall of photographs chronicled the history of the faculty. In the orientation session that was to come I would learn that my new school was one of the older and most reputable (by self acclamation) in North

America. In fact, it had a hundred-year history of excellence and we were all destined for greatness by association. As I continued to survey the graduation photographs looking for familiar Black dots to identify with, it seems the documented history of my people at this institution began in the early '80s with a lone Black student and would climax in 1997 with my graduating class of eleven Black students, the most the faculty had ever seen. I wonder what it was like for the first, the only, one of two, two out of one hundred, or the first Black woman. I wonder if they felt lucky, privileged, or like tokens. Did they struggle? Did they challenge or feel challenged? How did they survive? What were their secrets, their tools? How did they resist domination in an education system that is clearly not our own?

This memory causes me to reflect on my own journey through academia. I have witnessed programs unsuccessfully struggle to inte-grate racial, ethnic, and cultural content into curriculum. I have studied the disadvantaged, the marginalized, the cuturally different as if they were other forms of life. I have eaten free-range buffalo in an attempt to bring me one step closer to the Native experience. I have participated in the field trip to a "real" ethno-cultural agency to see how those people work with their community. I have sat painfully through the so-called anti-racism lectures which fail to address issues of white privilege and power, and the word racism is never uttered with diversity or multiculturalism being the safer topic. I have participated in arguments in which academic freedom was deemed a reasonable excuse for course content remaining racist and exclusionary.

While I wade through the madness of it all, I am intensely reminded that I am experiencing life as a Black female student from a marginal position in society. The margins being defined as how we as "minori-ties" experience reality, where we experience it, what we are allowed to experience, and what we can express as experience. At the same time I study how to look at my reality as a Black woman from outside its boundaries. It is a duality of existence. In one world, my location is that of object, to be studied, to be scrutinized and understood, to be assisted in a culturally-appropriate manner. In my world reality is defined through daily experiences of racism, sexism, and homophobia. These experiences are at the centre of my existence, my analysis. I use these experiences to challenge racist dominant culture, its paradigms and concepts which aim to negate my existence. In this duality, I am playing subject to my own objectification. I would venture to say that anyone who engages in learning while immersed in a culture other than their own will be confronted with fundamental questions of their own identity.

So, I am studying from an angle which doubles my vision. Outsider looking within and insider looking without. For this period of study, I am aware that I am accessing the knowledge of the so-called insiders, I am accessing their tools, something that was not a possibility for my ancestors and inaccessible to many of my present-day peers. I must learn to use this dual consciousness to negotiate through the contradictions that are to be resolved, my internalized self-definition as a Black woman, and my societal objectification as the marginalized other by my oppressors.

Knowledge is a social construction, controlled by power and authority. Those who have power in society define what is knowledge, they are the claim-makers and blessed are they who define how knowledge is constructed, legitimated, and used. These claims or "truths" then become what we in academe term the dominant discourse. It is this dominant discourse and those who benefit from its exclusionary suppression that are the targets of my resistance and challenge. I, as a Black woman studying in a white institution, am oppressed by the knowledge-base of dominant, European patriarchal discourse. I, like many of my colleagues and friends, have received the majority of my formal education in Canada and consider myself well-versed in the knowledge of the dominant culture. But this training is inadequate and flawed from my standpoint as a Black woman, a fact which I am reminded of daily in my counseling work with African clients who could not care less about how many degrees I have or where they were obtained. Their concern is how well I can help them negotiate a racist society. I struggle daily to challenge and overcome the contradictions that arise with what I am told is reality and what I experience as reality. I have to believe that my survival and my ability to express the totality of my experience cracks the foundation of the dominant discourse and its knowledge claims.

I also find myself trying to negotatiate a system in which knowledge is placed in a hierarchy, giving recognition and validation to the knowledge produced by some groups and denying the same privilege for others. My reality is based on the refuting and challenging of the knowledge and values of the white society which supports my position in the margins as the marginalized, as the oppressed, as the minority, in a world where people of colour make up more than half of the world's population. The tools I choose for assessing knowledge will be based on standards and criteria of my personal experience. How I conceptualize knowledge will determine how I define problems and eventually how I will intervene to find solutions. How is this empowering for those of us who experience oppression and, at the same time, powerful enough to subvert the actions of the oppressor? Resolving such a question not only involves self-reflection but also reflection on how I perceive my own racial identity. I need the support of my community to accomplish this task. I am not only a witness to individualized realities but also to the collective. Those of us who have been blessed with the opportunity to do so must responsibly create a voice for the often voiceless. As I write, I realize that as a writer you are creating an audience, therefore becoming as author. With authorship, I have authority and power and my experience and thought will be viewed as knowledge. I come from a culture based on oral traditions; the call and response of the drum, the amens from our church congregations. The challenge I face is to write, to study, to learn, and to pass on that knowledge in a manner that is free from domination, objectification, just a simple human encounter that is in keeping with my culture.

For us to voice our opposition to the imposed knowledge of racist formal education, we need to remove ourselves from the frameworks of the appointed authorities. For example, how different the single Black welfare mother would look if she was constructed from a Black woman's standpoint rather than the patriarchal racist media. Replacing the dominant culture's images with our own is an essential component in resisting the knowledge systems that create race, gender, sexuality, and class oppression. In order to make such a challenge, we need to use our own lives as evidence that the dominant view is weak. By self-definition we question not only what is reported about us, but also the credibility of the reporter. Through self-definition, we validate our existence, and we establish who has the authority to interpret our reality. By living and existing contrary to the portrayals created by white society, we extinguish the legitimacy of their claims. We, as Black women, are continually defined by outside forces who have no authority to do so. The negative stereotypes constructed by the dominant society run contrary to our realities, our culture, and our history. Self-definition and self-reliance not only empower us as the oppressed, but defiantly confront our oppressor.

Legitimate forms of equality can only be achieved through the understanding of human experience. The theories and knowledge and education of the dominant culture do not reflect the realities of my community, nor do they in any way convey our experiences. How effective can this knowledge then be if whole groups of people are rendered voiceless. The lives of people can not be understood through statistics, variables, or analyses which are based on a reality that does not match mine. If the knowledge base silences us, is it not safe to say that the methods used to assess this knowledge will do the same?

I explore these issues through the pain of racism as a Black student studying in a Eurocentric patriarchal system. Why, for example, am I penalized for referencing my Grandmother as an expert in an essay on Black women and labour and a notable academic suggested as an alternative source of information? Is my Grandmother's experience any less valid than the expert who has written a publishable document on the subject which fits the criteria laid out by a Eurocentric system? Once again, one must question whose knowledge is valued, who has access to such information, who has the ability to distribute such information and in what manner. I say I bear witness to my own suffering and can therefore elevate myself to the position of expert to that experience.

Although very difficult at times, through the recounting of deeply personal experiences, I can define myself while at the same time challenge the dichotomous nature of the dominant culture. Knowledge in that culture is hierarchical and value-laden. Emotion is pitted against reason and the experiential against theory. From this perspective one cannot be emotional and reasonable at the same time. We know that racism and matters of race are emotionally charged and according to this line of thinking, very personal accounts are seen without reason. How can you understand an experience by removing the emotional component of a story? Would this not render it useless in the construction of knowledge by those who experience discrimination daily?

Through the issue of experiential knowledge in my academic work, I have found an alternative knowledge base that provides a counter analysis to my objectification. Putting into practice the principle of self-definition, I believe it is an effective tool for social change and I would refute the idea that it needs to be assessed within the framework of the dominant culture to be validated. Does an experience need to be subjected to the rigours of statistical and analytical scrutiny to be legitimized? The recounting of a story not only empowers the writer but also those readers who have similar realities. The personal risk and sacrifices we have to make in order to secure social change are clear. The emotional upheaval, feelings of isolation, lack of understanding on the part of peers, and the enormous amount of energy required in the analysis of an experience are the things which legitimize one as an expert. One has lived the experience and can therefore articulate it with authority.

I, as a Black student on a Canadian campus, must come to terms at some point with the fact that I will interact with so few people who not only look like me, but sound like me. I have also had to come to terms with the fact that in order to succeed academically, I have had to employ the languages of those who hold positions of power over me personally, socially, and politically. As a Black student, you learn very quickly the value of the dominant language in comparison to your own reality and becoming bilingual is crucial for academic progress and survival. The investigation and understanding of the problems experienced by marginalized groups then requires more effort and creativity on my part which is not required by those students from the dominant culture. I must concern myself with not only interpreting and translating the language of my oppressors to fit into my reality, but must also ask, how do I empower others to seek alternative strategies which challenge the status quo? How does one effectively translate the knowledge gained from mainstream educational institutions into effective tools to understand, define, and create effective solutions for the oppressed? I think that self-exploration is the key. For me personally, understanding, focusing on, and sharing my experiences with others is, at times, difficult but also empowering. It highlights for me the fact that the most effective means of resistance can come from my own identity politics.

Mariel Belanger

Love Works Wonders

In the darkness
Before dawn
The land anticipates
The coming of a new day ...

How grateful it is
To be gently
Caressed
By the sun's rays

The flower worships
The sun by opening
Its petals full fledged
Growing with every
Touch

Love works wonders
Within nature and it
Does in mankind

For with all the sensations
Of the long awaited
Dawn
Is the anticipation
I feel for your embrace

Mariel Belanger

Native Child

Tell me a story
Teach me the ways of
The land
Guide me
Don't control me
Let me speak my mind
Hold me
Listen to me
Don't judge me
Care for who I am
Hear me
Understand me
I am your native child

Contributor Notes

Akidi-Pogo Abe was an Acholi woman activist, a poet, and a single mother. She was a member of the Ontario Board of Directors for Canadian Voice of Women for Peace and the coordinator of the African Women's Commission. A women's studies student at York University, she began writing poetry at the age of six, voicing the African woman's perspective and wisdom.

Kim Anderson is a Cree/Métis writer and educator. She is the principle consultant of her own firm, "The Write Circle," and the author of *A Recognition of Being: Reconstructing Native Womanhood* (Second Story Press, 2000). Kim lives in Guelph with her partner and their two children.

Mariel Belanger is a 26-year-old mother of two from the Okanagan Indian Reserve in Vernon, B.C. Her poetry is inspired by events in her life. She has been writing poetry since she was 14 years old and believes that people don't really know her until they read what is in her head, and, in her heart.

Dawn Burke is a native of Jamaica and is currently residing in Toronto. She is pursuing a Masters in Political Science at York University. Her research interests include political economy, gender relations, and development in the Caribbean. She is the founder and president of the Youth Educational Scholarship (YES) Foundation, a community-based organization providing scholarships for qualified Christian students attending accredited colleges and universities in Canada and the United States. Currently, she is the Program Specialist of the United Nations Development Fund for Women (UNIFEM) Caribbean Regional Office in Barbados. She writes as a means of self-expression and liberation.

Bishakha Chowdhury has done some work in shelters and group homes for wimmin. She strives to make the world a better place for all. Currently, she is a parent who is trying to live and raise her child (with her partner) as if the world is already that better place where all creation lives in love, respect, and harmony.

Tanya Cora is an English major at York University. She is of Jamaican and German heritage. She started writing poetry when she was 12 years old. For Tanya, the most interesting place to write is while riding the subway.

audra naomi diptee was born in Trinidad and Tobago but has been living in Canada since 1988. audra has been writing on and off since childhood.

Rolanda Elijah's native name is "Watwaniyost" (a good voice). She is a member of the Oneida Nation and an Environmental Studies student at York University. Twenty-seven years old, she is the mother of two girls and says her most powerful experience in life is motherhood.

Randa Hammadieh is a Muslim-Canadian of Syrian descent. Born in Windsor, Ontario, she grew up outside of Calgary, Alberta. She is currently in Political Science at the University of Toronto and aspires to a career in international law. Her source of inspiration in life is her parents.

Grisselda (Sophie) Harding is a 29-year-old student, activist, and writer. She was born in Jamaica and grew up in Canada. She resides in Toronto and is a student at York University. Her goal in life is to teach as well as to learn.

Rolanda Chavett Kane is a Nova Scotia-born articulate, universal, feminist, Black Poet. She has published poetry and writings in several journals, such as the *Halifax Daily News* special supplement to Black History Month 1994-1998, the *Dalhousie Gazette* 1994-1998. Currently, she is a member of The Black Artist's Network of Nova Scotia (BANNS) poets, playwrights, musicians, and performers. She is also a member of

The National Organization of Immigrants and Visible Minority Women of Canada (NOIVMWC) and a Local Advisory Committee Member of Immigrant and Visible Woman Organize Against AIDS.

Marisa Rosalind Maharaj is a 22-year-old student at Guelph University. Her permanent home is in Mississauga, Ontario where she lives with her mother. As for writing, all she can say is that she simply loves it. Through poetry especially she has found an outlet for her personal musings. This is her first publication.

Heather MacLeod, a Métis poet, was raised in the interior of British Columbia and is a graduate of the Creative Writing program at the University of Victoria. Some of her poetry has appeared in *Newest Review, Wascana Review, Fiddlehead, Grain, Prism International*, as well as in the anthologies *Breathing Fire* and *The Colour of Resistance*. Her first book of poetry, *My Flesh the Sound of Rain*, was released by Coteau in the autumn of 1998. Two of her plays have received honourable mentions from the journal *Aboriginal Voice* and from the Native Playwrights Contest held in Alaska. She has lived in British Columbia, Alberta, the Yukon, and Northwest Territories as well as in Turkey.

Marguerite, born Virma Benjamin, writes to dispel madness and preserve her sanity. After surviving five years in Peterborough, she currently lives in Toronto, working and completing a degree in public health. As a hedonistic Pisces, she is happiest enjoying life and her lover while being eternally grateful for family and true friends.

Notisha Massaquoi is currently negotiating the madness of Toronto while trying to find creative ways of acknowledging the lives of Black women through research, writing, and film. Professionally, she is the Health Promotion Coordinator of Women's Health in Women's Hands, a community health centre for women of colour.

Naomi North is currently a Vancouver-based mixed-race, comin' from poverty, survivor, feminist, femme dyke activist. The work included here is part of a process of developing a multi-media theatre performance by, about, and for survivors of child rape and sexual assault.

Mickie Poirier is an Algonquin Métis, born in Maniwaki, Quebec, on land that has since been returned to the Kitigan Zibi Reserve. She is a self-taught artist, in oils, painting mostly abstracts with her own personal twist, adding what she perceives to be the multi-universes of thought and emotion acting on matter. She lives a personal revolution against the anonymous, the "other-ness" of un-known names of un-known people.

Doreen Gaiyadéyéné:s Silversmith is a member of the Cayuga Nation and Six Nations Confederacy. She is a traditional Longhouse woman. A writer of short stories, poetry, and songs, she is currently working on her first book which she hopes to publish this fall. She is also a member of a Toronto-based Indigenous Women's Coalition and Women's Action Against Racist Policing.

Neeta Singh is the recipient of the Government of Canada's prestigious Commonwealth Scholarship and is currently pursuing her doctoral studies in the Department of English at York University. She is a previous recipient of the Jawahalal Nehru Memorial Award for her contribution to the field of literature in India where she obtained her M. Phil degree at the Jawahalal Nehru University. She has been both a political activist and a freelance journalist in India which inspired her to pursue post-colonial studies in Canada.

Lisa Nicole Tai is 23 years young. She is a Canadian of Chinese-Jamaican heritage. Markham, Ontario is the place she calls home. She is very spiritual, not so much religious. She believes in herself. She is a writer, in particular a poet; and she intends to forge a career out of being a professional writer. She is a Pisces. She loves food, both eating it and cooking it. She loves to dance. She loves all kinds of music, especially calypso and house. Her favourite colour is purple; it is the shade through which she sees the world. She tries not to take life too seriously. She is a dreamer.

Lorraine Thomas is 27 years old and is a First Nations Cree. She loves to read and write. She was born in Prince Albert Saskatchewan to Amy Thomas (Chamakese) and George Joseph (Kinematayo). She graduated from the Kelsey Siast Institute in 1997 and is currently enrolled in the education program at the University of Saskatchewan. She will have several poems and a short story entitled, "No Turning Back," published in a University of Saskatchewan anthology. She has had articles published in several newspapers and her poetry has appeared in two Canadian anthologies, *Images in Time* and *Glow Within*. She likes to write about her life on the trapline. She is also an aspiring actress. Her female role model is the angel of her life, her mother. Her hero is her father. Her male role model is her uncle, Lawrence Joseph, who is Second Vice Chief of the Federation, Saskatchewan, Indian Nation.

Roxane Tracey is a writer/visual artist who has loved the written word ever since she can remember. Her poetry has been published in the anthology, *Black Girl Talk*. In 1996, she developed the concept of "poetic art" which involves the fusion of Afrocentric images and inspirational poetry. This creative concept strives to awaken both the visual and mental senses while provoking insight and thought. Poetic Art™ can be seen online at: www.poeticartgallery.com

Vera M. Wabegijig is Anishnawbe-Kwe from Ontario and is 26 years old. "A lot of things can happen in three years. Since this submission, I now have a two-and-a-half-year-old daughter, Storm; I am in my second year of studies in Fine Arts at Victoria University; and I have had many poems published in anthologies including *Gatherings VIII & VIV, Native Women in the Arts* and *Breaking the Surface,* as well as an essay in *Reclaiming the Future: Women's Strategies for the 21st Century.* I give many thanks for my gift, many talents and support from my mother, Barbara, and my partner, Larry. P.S. We all await the new production in our family in August!"

Valerie Wood is an Ojibway woman. She lives in Barrie, Ontario with her partner, Mark and their children Taylor, Sarah, and Joshua. She is the Aboriginal Children's Program Worker at the Enaahtig Healing Lodge and Learning Centre in Victoria Harbour. In her spare time she enjoys reading, arts and crafts, and collecting children's literature.

Irene Young is from the Opasquiak Cree Nation which is in Northern

Manitoba. She has five beautiful children—Rhonda Ross, Gordie Bloomfield, Jennifer Dorion, Karla and Cheryl Bloomfield. The blessings from them are ten grandchildren. She is the resident Elder at the Assiniboine Community College in Brandon, Manitoba. She is currently employed by the Justice Department, Community and Youth Corrections, Norman Region, The Pas, Manitoba. Being a product of residential schools, Irene has had to overcome alcoholism, addictions, abuses (physical, mental, spiritual), and somehow manage to learn and retain the values and beliefs of her people.